Shaking the Wind

poems by

Matt Stefon

Finishing Line Press
Georgetown, Kentucky

Shaking the Wind

Copyright © 2017 by Matt Stefon
ISBN 978-1-63534-279-6 First Edition
All rights reserved under International and Pan-American Copyright Conventions.
No part of this book may be reproduced in any manner whatsoever without written permission from the publisher, except in the case of brief quotations embodied in critical articles and reviews.

ACKNOWLEDGMENTS

"Apotropaic" appeared in a self-published electronic chapbook, *The Long Contraction: Twelve Rejected Poems*, in November 2016.
"I wonder about the rain" appeared in *Babbling of the Irrational* on October 17, 2016.
"Kearney Square (Fragment)" appeared in *Oddball Magazine* on October 15, 2014.
"Lost bobber by the Merrimack" appeared in the Autumn 2016 issue of *Wilderness House Literary Review*.
"Me near the Breakwater (P-Town, 6/21/08)" appeared in the Summer 2016 issue of *Coup D'Etat*.
"Sincerity" appeared in the *Penmen Review* on September 15, 2016.

Most of these poems also were read by me in short "poemfilms" that appear on my YouTube channel. The poemfilm of "Injuring Eternity at Boott Mills" was also featured on the blog of the literary journal *Dirty Chai* on May 3, 2016.

Publisher: Leah Maines

Editor: Christen Kincaid

Cover Art: Matt Stefon

Author Photo: Matt Stefon

Cover Design: Elizabeth Maines McCleavy

Printed in the USA on acid-free paper.
Order online: www.finishinglinepress.com
also available on amazon.com

Author inquiries and mail orders:
Finishing Line Press
P. O. Box 1626
Georgetown, Kentucky 40324
U. S. A.

Table of Contents

Whatever gives birth to poetry 1

Sincerity 2

Injuring Eternity at Boott Mills 4

Apotropaic 5

I wonder about the rain 7

Lost bobber by the Merrimack 8

Tulpa 9

A voided tree 10

Lunch break at the temp job 11

The Shiners 12

Rush hour in Newmarket 13

A bent rainbow 14

Just near twilight, Mid-November 15

The coming dark 17

Kearney Square (Fragment) 18

Me near the Breakwater (P-Town, 6/21/08) 19

Whatever gives birth to poetry

Dawn will not
give you back
a greeting
and soft word
persuasion
is useless
as old shit
dropped down to
fertilize
nothing and
just covers
everything,
all slick and
pervasive.
As much as
I'd like I
can't help here.
You might try
shaking the
wind. Use the
teeth sitting
in your mouth.
Hold it there
till its hurt
is your hurt—
the same hurt—
till both hurt
like twilight
exuded
there when dawn's
head pokes through.

Sincerity
for Minori and for I-495, which always gets us home

If you lay your heart bare
earlier than the trees in mid-October,
you should prepare for cold.
They're still wearing orange,
red, and yellow school sweatshirts
over their trunks for some
time after graduation,
and will do so till they've become
fully acclimated to the
chilly work mornings after summer goes.

You can see them queued up
along 495 before you hit Lawrence
bending in the orange sun,
shaking just a bit beneath their shirts
as if investigating the plausible existence
of tickets for the Fall Classic
because someone gave their word
somewhere on social media
and the promise it was true
was too good to resist.

You, however, are much like me,
despite standing on the other
side of agreement, all too ready
without reticence to drink in so early
the ice cold integrity of orange juice.
Or, rather, you are how
I used to be before
I got attuned to the working world
showing its whitening years
before the full reveal.

Steering the Civic
with one sweatshirted arm,
I reach the other your way
to turn the heater on,
acclimated far better
than you are to
another frosty morning of
negotiating traffic,
red and yellow giving
only orange consolation.

Injuring Eternity at Boott Mills

Maybe because it first had to convert
to unemployment from employment like
so many other souls in Merrimack
Valley and beyond, the brick that makes up
the cradle here of our Industrial
Revolution is browning, and, despite
the Park Service's efforts, wearying.
This despite a new conversion into
a new being—something useful. Influx
and efflux of tourist upon tourist,
class trip on class trip—it wears a body,
out, even if of formidable brick
instead of the less sterner stuff (aren't
bodies overrated, it's been said?). Well,
having nowhere particular to go
on a sunny Saturday morning, at
the end of a wicked brutal work week
myself, I sit at a table planted
outside just for me (and any other
tenant passing through here—I live here now),
drink coffee with maple, and watch old oaks
whisper in the silent breeze and other
fellow tenants headed up to the lot
to have their cars take them up or down the
shore (doesn't really matter), not really
thinking let alone caring that like me
and the trees and the mill they were really
implicated just now in killing time.

Apotropaic

The first sunrise after the year's shortest night brings
a cold satisfaction to the unfolding course of things.
Now begins the long contraction,
though logic has it rising twenty-five degrees by lunch,
and despite the growing season. The truth is, time
isn't something to anxiously
check on your iPhone over your coffee
to know how much longer before
breakfast passes into lunchtime
(even though that is a valid reason to hold your interest).
It's a projected dissatisfaction
with the inevitable folding of all things
toward their source.

We reasonably say we have some good
more days to invest before then.
(It suits our interest.) The Solstice
promises boundless growth and harvest, while in fact
summer starts shutting down early
even though things stay open late.
This promise: inevitably a protection
with a logic turning away all the bad thought
like a calm breeze blowing dandelion seed.
Yet the plain truth that can't be refuted
is that all the preparations leading up to
Independence Day only lead
to infuriating complacency.

Tell yourself what you like. I do it too.
But the inevitable exchange of coolness for warmth
is what logic says we have to look forward to.
Only dissipation and transition.
No debts (without interest) are ever really paid.

Your skin will never really be warmed.
Your belly will never be really full.
Why not then turn back to the hard truth of things?
This is really all that needs to be:
When confronted with another's suffering
don't pick apart and scrutinize the reasons.
Unfold your head and heart like the season.
Fold your rationalizations
into yourself.

I wonder about the rain
for Robert Creeley

Awoken to grey
pouring in my
window
with the sound
of the tin sky
slopping
all over the
ground—

The sloppiness
outside at first
sounds as
if coming from
the other side,
but where
the toy car and
tin pan sound?

And if I go
into that pouring
sloppiness—
that outside world
silently slickening
with
persistent
sound

of tinned beans
spilling into
breakfast,
slopping onto the
dull tin plate
under the dull tin
sky—how can
I keep clean?

Lost Bobber by the Merrimack

Cast out from the bank
it drops from the branch—
neon orange yellow—
indicating better fishing
elsewhere.

Gray water below
it droops on the line—
tiny plastic spider
caught upon a proud, horrendous
gallows.

Swaying from its foot—
a drizzle of silk
out into the ether—
final record of some shot at
pleasure.

Tulpa

Sprung out my head
like new trauma
on the block when
a fire burns out

and night pours in—
if you find the
incantation
that wrung you here—

in being—wanting,
here's form to this:
authority's
a sung fiction—

new, trembling thing,
doesn't yet know
why it was born—
neither do I—

A voided tree

At least the ground
can start to heal
at last from the
nurturing
it long gave.

Remember that
this winter when
you're burning what
this ground was
nurturing.

Lunch break at the temp job

The pesticide
sting of chlorine
pricks you first. Out
on the beeless

lawn one billion
needles stand green
to stick you back
should you step on

them. The trick to
this whole half-hour:
eat your fill of
sun-baked blacktop

in the eggshell
sky. A hungry
bird, by hunger
triggered, shoots north.

The Shiners

Pop (my grandfather) dumped the foam bait pail
at the edge of the woods when we got to
Harris Pond, and they all without a wail
came pouring out. "There's nothing we can do,"
he said in that voice tone meant to instruct
an eight-year-old in rule of law's finer
odds-and-ends. He put a lure on the duct-
tape-handled pole. I stood, watched each shiner
gasp wordless where I stood at the woods' edge,
iridescent droplets doing no good
outside a pond. If I could speak, I'd hedge
a bet (too late now) that we maybe should
have gone another place to try our luck.
The sign said it. "No Live Bait." We were stuck.

Rush hour in Newmarket

The construction
on 108
where they ripped up
all the blacktop

so they could lay
down new blacktop
isn't the worst
part. Now you have

to drop it all
for this evening's
inconvenience
of being stuck dead

still in a stopped
car on opened
earth among a
glum procession.

A bent rainbow
> *for Dylan and for Dover*

The light, dying, dinged the rainclouds
that had rolled in above Dover
and had closed up like an iron vest
and then would not part after the
rain let up. If the sun had just
not gone so far down it may have
given something more to us than
one seven-shade beam to hold back
the storm's remnants—and we saw that
from beneath the windows in the
consolation of the twilight
falling. That's it. And then in our
desolation we saw that was
bent—gravity had got it too.

Just near twilight, mid-November

when the moon
with its skull
socket eyes
beams over the
Piscataqua
white against
the blue
rising over
the bridge over
to Maine
I am driving
on the Spaulding
behind the
windshield
under it all
and I'm glancing
out the window
on the side
where my wife
sits sleeping
seat slumped back
after a long
day of life
and work and
is so peaceful
with the still
Seacoast and the
Piscataqua
sliding under
the bridge to
Maine
or rather

I should say
"was" sliding
"was" still
"was" peaceful
"was" driving
"was" beaming
("did" beam?)
because now
we're home and
there's another
type of
window
between us
and the moon

The coming dark

A couple coffeehouse lights still press
the night back to the windows inside—
outside, Market Street deepens to a purple
almost the blue of the brick in the
credit union across the street, one light

in the ATM. Maybe there's
something to be wary of, if not worried
about, even though I know the neighborhood.
I've never come really to know the dark

all that well—just that after night goes, morning
comes, then another night, an obtrusive
acquaintance. I'm tired of acquaintances
streaming past out there, away from the grinders
and steamers hushing the day toward close.

Kearney Square (Fragment)
for Boston

It's not that love is showing its gold
like the honey locust trees in mid-August
      and the sun they catch at seven.

This isn't one of those mornings of late
that staunched the sky like a terrier gray
      sweatshirt after a jog.

The recent construction has made known all
the pipes and bricks and wires that enweb
      the whole neighborhood.

The Sunscraper, too, was showing the mortar
it keeps beneath the august facade
      of creamy deco.

Market Street doesn't usually grant me
this much inspiration, even in the morning,
      so I'll take what I can get.

Me near the Breakwater (P-Town, 6/21/08)

She, who loves you, and whom you love as well,
snapped on the disposable Kodak bought
at CVS downtown before you got
to the inn, you seeming to soften, melt,
evaporate, with the hazy morning,
the white strand foregrounding the distance there.
Why would she do that? Keep you standing there?
Obviously to keep all that morning
whole, fresh, and to keep you with it, to keep,
even after check out, you for a while.
Otherwise you could have melted farther
into the horizon: lighthouse, houses,
the sand swallowing you like a cod cake...
like the slug of time in the ferry's wake.

Additional Acknowledgments

I owe deep debts of gratitude for this book even entering existence at all, and I'll keep this modest attempt at satisfying the deepest of them brief. I thank my wife, Minori Haga Stefon, my parents, Frederick and Christine, and my sister, Jessica, for their love and encouragement. I want to thank my first teacher in poetry, David Chin, for showing me how to vanquish what I can only call the edgelordy high school romanticism that infected my earliest attempts at verse. I want to thank all of my friends for their support, but I want to thank four in particular: Brandon E. Beck, Jose Pedro Zuquete, Michael Balticzar Katz, and Chelsey Parrott-Sheffer. In various degrees of support, they've been the best friends my poetry has had. There are several institutions that deserve thanks, but above all, I must thank Brew'd Awakening Coffeehaus in Lowell, Massachusetts, and in particular those working there between 2013 and 2015, the period when I was a most regular regular, performed my first poetry open mic and slam, and wrote at least the notes that subsequently became many of these poems. Thanks also to Untitled Open Mic, held at Brew'd, for creating such a welcoming space in which to recite and try out poems. Thank you all.

Matt Stefon lives and writes north of Boston. He studied English, American studies, and history at Penn State and religious studies, Chinese and comparative philosophy and religion (with an interest in comparison between Confucianism and neo-Confucianism, American Transcendentalism, and the philosophical theology of Bernard M. Loomer), and American and comparative literature at Boston University.

He taught English and humanities at Middlesex Community College for several years, served as religion editor of *Encyclopaedia Britannica* for eight years, teaches comparative religion in Norwich University's online degree completion division, and serves as associate editor of poetry for *West Texas Literary Review*.

His film criticism has appeared in *Killing the Buddha* and in *Journal of Religion and Film*. poems have appeared in *Oddball Magazine, Three Line Poetry, the Unrorean, Coup D'Etat, the Penmen Review, Babbling of the Irrational, Wilderness House Literary Review,* and *Poppy Road Review*.

He also makes short "poemfilms" of his poems and of select favorite classic poems, and uploads them to his YouTube channel. He has self-published three short ebooks of poetry: *The Long Contraction: Twelve Rejected Poems; Winter: Four Poems;* and *Incandescent Nothing: Short Poems and Aborted Lyrics*. This is his first print collection.

www.ingramcontent.com/pod-product-compliance
Lightning Source LLC
LaVergne TN
LVHW041525070426
835507LV00013B/1834